tldr
a diary of poems

Elizabeth Goldie

Presentation by *BookLeaf Publishing*

Web: www.bookleafpub.com

E-mail: info@bookleafpub.com

ISBN: 9789358369656

First edition 2023

DEDICATION

to those who dare to dream

ACKNOWLEDGEMENT

First of all, I want to thank myself for not letting myself get in the way of finishing this book. Sometimes, we are our own worst enemy, and the fact that this collection exists proves that I haven't fallen victim to my own consciousness. Yet.

Secondly, I want to thank my parents, family, and friends for every ounce of support and encouragement they've given me. The loud (and silent) cheers have meant the world to me, and I will treasure every bit of love they have poured into me.

And lastly, to the reader, I hope this poetic journey was something you could relate to. Thank you for taking it with me.

every now and then

every now and then,
i stumble across a quiet moment.
i cradle it in my hands,
and tuck it away in my heart,
keeping it safe.

every now and then,
i slip into a moment so perfect,
i can't help but reach out and grasp it,
sealing it away in my soul,
preserving it forever.

every now and then,
i remember my little treasures,
and pull a stolen memory out.
watching as the flickering reel plays out,
and once again, everything is okay.

alone

often, i find myself wishing
that i was alone.
until i am.

i wish to sit in my own company,
content with my things,
quiet and peaceful.

yet, i know i long for the company of others,
that i crave the possibility of memories,
the laughter and chaos.

but i'm merely a backup,
there to take the seat of those unable to come,
a placeholder on standby.

the one behind the camera,
the one that walks on the grass,
the one always forgotten.

so i sit, and i tell myself,
it's okay,
i like being alone.

but i can't help but wish,

that for once,
i was included too.

leave your message at the tone

"hey,
    it's me.
        again."
i choke back a laugh,
feel it stick in my throat,
plug up all the words i have so carefully planned
out.

"i just…
    i just wanted to say hey, and
maybe see how you're doing."

i pause and draw in a breath,
so weighted and heavy,
the phone now so leaden.

"i'm okay, things are okay…"

it's so hard to swallow,
and everything is sluggish and slow
and i squeeze my eyes shut.
a single stupid tear escaping
as the words i've held captive in my heart
force their way out into the bated silence

and…

"i miss you."

my voice is so foreign.
so frail and shaky and timid.
my heart pounds viciously in my chest
and i swear it begins to crack
as the words pour out of me;
wonky and disjointed,
then all at once,
like a restrained flood let loose.

"i'm sorry,
     i promised myself
i wouldn't get emotional,
     but here i am.
     calling you,
                    again."

"wishing that you'd pick up,
     wishing it would go back to normal.
          wishing that we could go back to
normal."

something inside me fractures
at the mention of "we".
there is no we,
or us, or ours.

it's over, and i know it,
but i can't shut up
and i just wish you knew that-

"i miss you.
everyday, i miss you.
        and i am so,
                so sorry.
        for everything.
                    for all of it."

i'm not standing anymore.
i'm a crumbling,
dissolving,
shattering mess
on my kitchen floor
as my throat constricts
and i can't suppress my childish sniffling
as i whisper,

        "i hope you're okay."

the silence stretches on,
and i realize a beat too late that
the recording has ended.
the message is sent
and my last chance to tell you has slipped away.
my last chance to tell you that,

"i love you."

a plea,
a confession,
a desperate wish mouthed
into the deafening silence of a room
filled with despair.
and as the phone slips out of my hand
and clatters so harshly against the ancient
linoleum floor,
my pathetic little heart finally gives out,
and breaks into
a million
irreparable
fragments.

nostalgia

nostalgia creeps like a vine across ancient
bricks.
it carves rivets into records,
and collects dust on shelves.
slowly bleeding its scent into candle wax.

it lies in wait,
drumming its cool fingers together,
patient and cunning,
striking at just the right moment.

it's there,
evident in the twist in your heart,
the fog over your mind.
it's the single, agonizing memory,
that rises to the surface,
breaking the beauty of memories
into a fine dust of melancholia.

nostalgia locks out all that is,
blots out the light of the moment,
and leaves behind
only the skeleton of what once was.

it's the patronizing, pathetic pain

that sears through
the film of everything peaceful,
and crushes the heart
slowly
with each single,
sad note.

nostalgia.
hidden in the crevices of your soul,
is either your savior,
or your ghost.

sometimes i feel

sometimes, i feel so
angry.
like the rage bubbles up
from the depths of my soul
and spills out my lips,
spreads through my veins,
spears my limbs and heart,
and seizes my mind.

sometimes, i feel so,
sad.
like the intensity of my hurt
grips the entirety of my being,
so heavy and burdensome,
so listless and despondent,
a dull ache occupies the hole in my chest.

sometimes, i feel so,
useless.
like my entire purpose is
to offset the lives of those around me,
a comparative that at least
they are not
me.

sometimes, i feel so,
afraid.
like time is slipping,
sliding, spinning out of control,
away from me,
leaking out the fabric of space
and escaping into the void.

sometimes, i feel so,
stupid.
like i can't grasp the simplest of things,
i can't recite or create or inspire,
i feel like a cracked vessel,
a discarded, fractured piece,
too broken to be repaired.

sometimes, i feel as though,
i will never be enough.
so, i sit and wish,
that all the depths of my feelings,
could for once,
serve a purpose.

ghost

sometimes, in the still seconds before the world
comes crashing down,
you can feel the ghost of the person you once
were, watching.

sometimes, in the frozen moment between now
and forever,
the world rewinds and everything is as it once
was.

sometimes, hiding in the cracks of your heart,
lies a whisper of melancholia, poised to
suffocate your soul.

 sometimes, the past swallows the present,
only for a solitary second.

sometimes, the film of memories flickers by,
each scene is a glimpse of a time long since
gone.

and sometimes, in those few quiet, static,
seconds,
the entirety of eternity is decided.

leaden

That one sinking feeling,
That turns leaden in your stomach;
Winds its leathery fingers around your throat
And squeezes your lungs
Spreading its spindly tendrils across your heart,
Whispering in your ear and stroking your
shoulders,
Trailing along your skin, leaving goosebumps in
its wispy wake.
That one sinking feeling that captures your soul.
Is it merely returning,
taking up residence in your fractured heart?
Or did it never leave since the start?

over-stim-u-late-d

My skin feels too tight,
The world is too loud,
And the light too bright.

Fade in,
Fade out,
Watch the scenery start to spin.

Cling to consciousness,
Feel reality slip,
Fight the urge to wither into distress.

I can't remember,
Where this starts,
Or where it ends.

But I wish it would be over,
Before the chaos
Sinks in.

insignificant

that moment, frozen in time
when your heart drops, crumbles
slips out of your chest and onto the floor
trampled underfoot, as you stand
invisible and motionless
unimportant and unwanted
a waste of space in a room full of people

the moment, when you realize
how insignificant you are
how no one needs you,
wants you,
notices you
you're just
invisible

that moment, here and gone
they don't remember you
your face, your laugh, your smile
you don't matter, outside of that split second
outside of the bubble of casual conversation
you are nothing
immemorable
utterly, hopelessly, torturously, insignificant

your wants, hopes, dreams
insignificant
your feelings, anxieties, concerns
insignificant
your face, your laugh, you
insignificant

and when they do notice you
it's pity
pity for the sad lost soul sitting in the corner.

edge of eternity

tick
    tick
        tick
second after second,
slipping between the spidery cracks on the
clock;
sliding down the wall,
melting away, dissolving into puddles of idle
talk.

tick
    tick
        tick
sun rise, sun set
        day's gone, reset.
broken pencils, torn paper, a discarded wrapper.
time steps slowly, success's kidnapper.

tick
    tick
        tick
a second into an hour into a day into a week
        the world treks on, the outlook bleak.
it's there and then gone, the joy of living,

wisps of a memory evaporating at the edges of a
mind unforgiving.

tick

        tick…

a moment wasted, a word left unsaid,
        an almost, trailing the wake of thoughts
and wishes laid upon their deathbed.
        the present, a slow torturous, mindfully
crazed descent.
the impending future crushing the few precious
seconds still left,
        stealing every second, slipping it away.
 melting each moment into another
mind-numbing day.

tick

and it's gone.
just like that, the clock strikes on.
        forbidden wishes, drowning in the sea of
time.
left in the withered hands of souls without
rhyme.
        souls whose delicate resolves crumbled
beneath opportunities forgotten,
eternally behind, alone, desolate, and rotten.

...

so, hurry, escape.
flee the clutches of this second.
find harmony and live on the blurred lines of its
landscape,
        in the place where broken hearts mend.

sorrow, solace, and spite

sorrow, solace, and spite.
the three guardians of words,
stand resolute at the gates of our mouths,
perched and poised to wreak havoc, bring peace,
or destroy.

sorrow,
stabbing,
like a blade in your back,
twisting, slicing you open,
blood dripping from between each crack.

solace,
soothing,
like cool water on a blistering day,
a means of comfort,
rinsing every hurt away.

spite,
irritating,
like sand in your eyes,
painful and bothersome,
pulling patience apart with excruciating cries.

sorrow, solace, spite.
forlorn and lovely and cunning.
they ring in harmony with the chaos of the earth,
oxymorons within their own right,
altering the courses of life.

they can mean nothing at all.
they can sit, idle and useless, merely letters,
strewn across a page, a screen, a wall,
but they are always, always, intentional
in who they choose to become their debtors.

sorrow, solace, and spite.
the three guardians to the gates of our mouths.
meant for damage, for love, for malice,
they can shatter, mend, or separate
the pieces of a broken heart.

i promised myself

i promised myself,
i wouldn't fall in love again.
and yet, here i sway,
on the edge of another dizzying fall.

where i'll land,
i don't know just yet.
but hopefully,
you're there too.

i can't stop it,
my heart keeps running ahead.
leaping over every shred of reason i have left,
so desperate to keep you.

i want you to stay,
i want to spend every moment of forever by your
side.
but i can't help but remember,
that i promised myself,

i wouldn't fall in love again.

love isn't enough

sometimes,
it doesn't matter
how much you love them.
love isn't
enough.

love is not enough
to hold two people
together.

love is not enough
to keep two hearts
aligned.

love without consequence,
love without action,
love without intention,
is never,
enough.

you might think
you know their heart.
inside
and out.

and yet,
you don't.
you can't.
and you never will.

because nothing lasts forever.
it falls apart,
and sometimes,
it cannot be fixed.

stuck

paralyzed by your own mind,
trapped within the confines of your
consciousness,
bound and subject to your thoughts;
a captive in your own body.

here, in the eye of the storm,
an undercurrent of chaos bubbles,
jolting and nervous,
it flows hot and cold, hot and cold.

urging you to rush,
hurry, get up and go,
for time marches onward,
without you.

but bound and subject to your mind,
you remain,
trapped and unable to move,
a prisoner within the temple of your awareness,
as the world steps on
without you.

the fool

always the fool,
left behind,
forgotten and invisible,
melting into the wall as the evening fades.

always the fool,
watching as they laugh,
as they live their lives,
make memories to last forever.

always the fool,
stuck and alone,
insignificant,
a ghost.

always the fool,
listening as it the call goes to voicemail,
waiting as the silence washes over me,
remembering, that i promised myself

i wouldn't be here again
desperate to matter,
desperate to be
anything but the fool.

it's okay

"it's okay"
a gentle whisper,
hanging delicately in the air,
balanced tentatively,
waiting with bated breath.

so soft and tender,
a heart cradled in calloused palms,
lovingly held, safe and sound.

"it's okay"
engulfed, encircled, enveloped.
soothed by the steady, eased by the consistent.
safe, in this space between souls.
safe in this sanctuary between bodies.

"it's okay"
the sirens sound,
the world begins to crumble.
piece by piece,
it dissolves into pools of nothingness.

but this remains.
so dainty, so sacred, so precious,
is the love blossoming between the fractures

of two hearts once broken.

restless is a soul without love,
in-complete is a life without compassion,
unhappy is a heart without light.

but here, consoled by the quiet amidst the chaos,
secure, safe, serene,
soothed and held,
it's okay.

she is

sunkissed, effervescent, sparkling, and bubbly
she's champagne on a summer's night,
the twinkle of the first evening star.

she's effortless and reckless,
all windblown hair and scattered freckles,
carefree laughter and boundless creativity.

she walks with such confidence,
she speaks with such animation,
she's enrapturing.

she is kind,
she is caring,
she is love and joy and peace.

she is color and life and light,
she is everything i ever wished to be,
and she is.

because from the depths of despair,
a mosaic of a thousand broken pieces arose,
each one a lesson, each fragment placed there by
my own bleeding hands.

a culmination of every hardship, heartbreak, and
heaven,
held within the borders of a smile,
beautiful, bubbling, bursting with hope.

a future filled with infinite possibilities,
renewed, refreshed, revived through every
struggle,
brimming with potential, a new beginning.

and as i watch her,
through the looking glass of those i love,
i realize,
she always was, and will always be,
beautiful.

the sliver of space between hearts

oh, the magic of a first kiss,
the tender, stolen brush of lips
gentle and nervous,
butterflies and quick breaths.

fingertips graze your jaw,
slip into your hair,
pull you in closer,
two bodies pressed together.

how the heart stops,
the world slows,
and time freezes,
and there is nothing but this.

fragile and new,
incredible and exciting,
uncharted territory unfolding
in the sliver of space between hearts.

looking glass

you can sit,
and gaze upon a shooting star,
and whisper a silent prayer
to the looming sky above,

and you can sit,
and stare out upon the ocean,
and admire the strength in its waves,
and the grace of its curves,

and you can observe,
the towering elegance of the mountains,
the dips and valleys and peaks and slopes,
and the beauty of its steely presence,

and you can touch the ripples in a lake,
feel the prick of pine needles beneath your bare
feet,
taste the salt breeze off the coast,
see the magnificence of a horizon undisturbed,

but you can never
bring into fruition,
or wish into existence,
or find in the world,

a being as unique and beautiful,
as yourself.

moment by moment

there are moments,
every now and then,
sprinkled throughout the mundane,
that are almost too perfect.

when the sky is clothed in orange and pink,
when there's a sale on a desperately wanted
item,
when a chorus of laughter fills the air,
when everything is safe and happy and right.

there are moments,
every now and then,
left scattered between every golden memory,
when the world seems to quiet and fade out.

when the night sky is lit up by lightning bugs,
or bouquets of wildflowers seem to brighten the
room.
when the car windows are down and the stereo
volume is up,
or the soft comfort of blankets on a rainy day.

there are moments,
every now and then,

hidden in-between the bustle of life,
that stay sealed in your heart forever.

the way your heartbeat stuttered when you heard
the news,
the bumbling excitement over a first date,
the deep quiet when all alone in the middle of
the night,
the anxious anticipation of a big day ahead.

there are moments,
every now and then,
that temper the rest of life's chaos,
and remind us that

we remember
not days,
but moments.

silence

at the end of the day,
when the sun sinks below the horizon,
the bustle dissolves into a faint hum,
the silence settles, thick and heavy.

left in the dark quiet,
everything returns, haunting and sweet,
and reminds me of the small moments left
untouched,
until uncovered in that stillness.

sometimes, the pain seeps in,
slipping between the tender creases in my fragile
memory,
taking up residence in the murky fragments,
searing through my heart and veins.

the melancholic ache sets in,
soft and heavy,
intoxicating and vast in its reach,
and i sit, watching everything play over and over
again.

through the memories,
i live.

dissecting them, frame by frame,
until i am surrounded by the skeletons of the
moments i love most.

fine

9 789358 369656